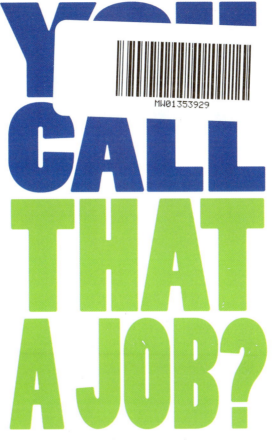

YOU CALL THAT A JOB?

Patrick Daley

PHOTO CREDITS Cover: © Underwood & Underwood/Corbis; pp. 2–3: © Richard Cummins/Corbis; p 4: © Nancy Rica Schiff/Odd Jobs; p. 5: © Kevin Morley/ Corbis; p 6: © Markku Lahdesmaki/Corbis; p 7: © Jeffrey L. Rotman/Corbis; p. 8: © Anthony Bannister/Gallo Images/Corbis; p 9: © David R. Frazier Photo library Inc./Alamy; p 10: © Reuters/Corbis; p 11: © Tom Wagner/Corbis; p 12: © Underwood & Underwood/Corbis; p 13: © Hulton-Deutsch Collection/Corbis; p 14: © Touhig Sion/Corbis Sygma/Corbis; p 15t: © Michael Coglianty /Getty Images, c: © Archive Holdings Inc./Getty Images.

No part of this publication may be reproduced in whole or in part, or stored in a retrieval system, or transmitted in any form or by any means, electronic, mechanical, photocopying, recording, or otherwise, without written permission of the publisher. For information regarding permission, write to Scholastic Inc., 557 Broadway, New York, NY 10012.

Copyright © 2006 by Scholastic Inc.
All rights reserved. Published by Scholastic Inc. Printed in the U.S.A.

ISBN 0-439-74037-1

SCHOLASTIC, SCHOLASTIC FX BOOKS, and associated logos and designs are trademarks and/or registered trademarks of Scholastic Inc.

LEXILE is a registered trademark of MetaMetrics, Inc.

5 6 7 8 9 10   40   13 12 11 10

SCHOLASTIC INC.
New York   Toronto   London   Auckland   Sydney   Mexico City   New Delhi   Hong Kong   Buenos Aires

Dear Reader:

"Time to work. You'd better <u>prepare</u>.
You've got to get a job!" said my old Aunt <u>Claire</u>.

I hopped on the bus. I had the right <u>fare</u>.
I went by myself. I traveled solitaire.

I <u>saw</u> a lot of jobs. How did they <u>compare</u>?
Some of them took training. <u>All</u> of them took care.

I saw good jobs, hard jobs, jobs that <u>scare</u>.
Some jobs I'd take, but others—I wouldn't <u>dare</u>!

Now tell me what YOU think. I think it's only <u>fair</u>.
You call that a job . . . or a job <u>nightmare</u>?

Patrick Daly

Statue Cleaner

Look up there. Check out that <u>dude</u>.
He's cleaning out her ear. He's not being <u>rude</u>.

Statues get dirty. To keep them looking <u>new</u>,
he scrubs and scrubs. He just can't overdo.

This may not be the right job for you.
But you've got to admit, he's got a world-class view!

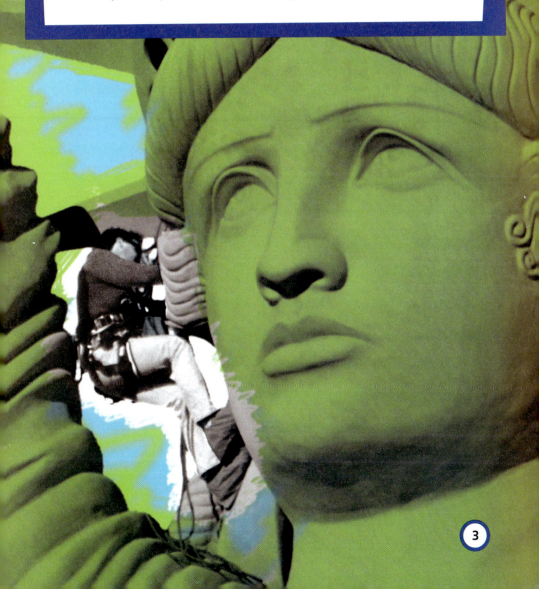

Deodorant Tester

It's her job! It's not her fault.
She's looking for smells. The ones that assault.

A smell from a pit assaults her nose.
In a job like this—anything goes!

It doesn't matter. She doesn't despair.
She fills out a report and a questionnaire.

After work, she does declare,
"Get me out of here. I need fresh air!"

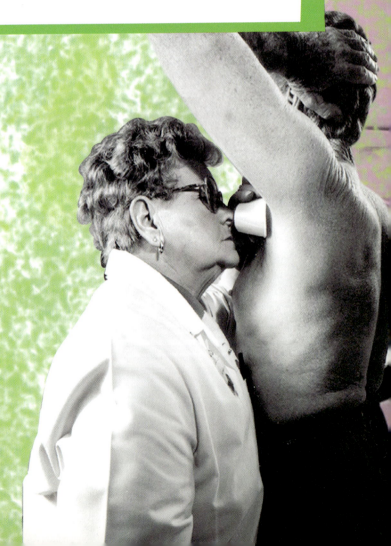

Video Crew

Zoom in. Zoom out. Lower the boom.
This video crew is working in a tiny bathroom.

Why, you wonder? Were you not aware?
This bathroom won a contest. No others compare.

Zoom in. Zoom out. Get close to the bowl.
Get the best shot. That's the goal!

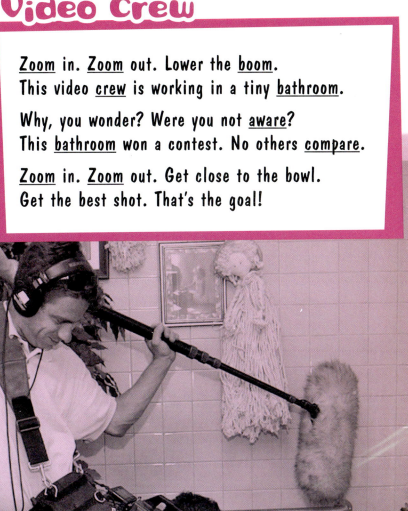

Shopping Cart Collector

He <u>crawls</u> out of bed at the crack of <u>dawn</u>.
He's <u>aware</u> of the time. Yet he barely <u>yawns</u>.

He's out to round up some shopping carts
That shoppers nabbed from the grocery mart.

Sure, taking carts is against the <u>law</u>.
But some shoppers don't care. "That <u>law</u> has a <u>flaw</u>!"

"Our bags are heavy. We have too far to <u>walk</u>.
We need to borrow those carts! We have a right to <u>balk</u>."

"We need these carts. We have meals to <u>prepare</u>.
This is an <u>assault</u>. It's cart <u>warfare</u>!"

But the man doesn't bother with the shopping cart <u>brawl</u>.
He just <u>hauls</u> the carts back to the shopping <u>mall</u>.

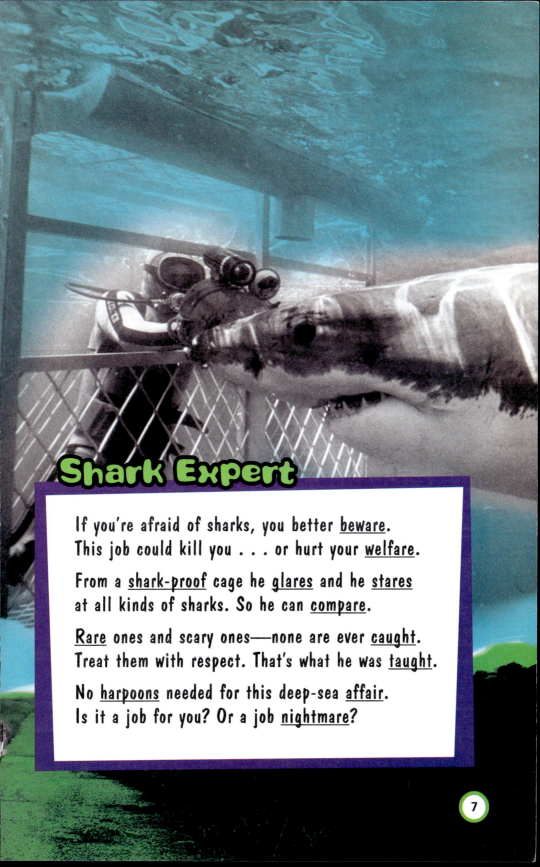

Shark Expert

If you're afraid of sharks, you better <u>beware</u>.
This job could kill you . . . or hurt your <u>welfare</u>.

From a <u>shark-proof</u> cage he <u>glares</u> and he <u>stares</u>
at all kinds of sharks. So he can <u>compare</u>.

<u>Rare</u> ones and scary ones—none are ever <u>caught</u>.
Treat them with respect. That's what he was <u>taught</u>.

No <u>harpoons</u> needed for this deep-sea <u>affair</u>.
Is it a job for you? Or a job <u>nightmare</u>?

Snake Handler

This isn't a job for the weak or immature.
You probably won't find it in a Cool Jobs brochure.

He's a snake-poison milker. That's the truth.
He's been working with snakes since the days of his youth.

Doctors make use of all he <u>withdraws</u>.
They use it in their research—this poison from the <u>jaws</u>!

Working with snakes has one <u>downfall</u>.
If you get bit too <u>often</u>, it's a total close <u>call</u>!

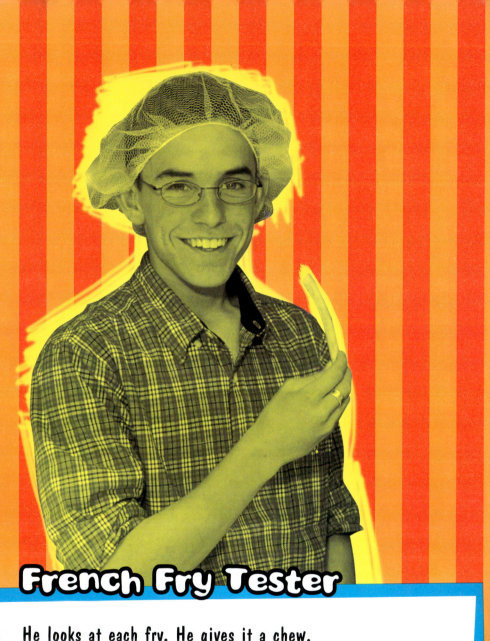

French Fry Tester

He looks at each fry. He gives it a <u>chew</u>.
It's really a job. Can you imagine? Who <u>knew</u>?

Are they good enough? Thick enough? What's his point of view?
He's not going to tell you. You need to read his review.

Ostrich Farmer

She raises these birds on her massive farm.
She keeps them well fed. She keeps them from harm.

They can't fly away. And we can <u>conclude</u> . . .
they don't mind the weather or the high <u>altitude</u>.

You assume she's crazy? She's <u>off</u> the <u>wall</u>?
I can assure you. She's not at <u>all</u>.

She wants to retire. She will real <u>soon</u>.
She's made a lot of money.
She's an ostrich <u>tycoon</u>!

Video Game Tester

Check it out. Try it out. Give it a review.
What do you think? Is this an awesome job for you?

Which games are best? State your point of view.
The <u>bosses</u> are looking for big <u>revenue</u>.

They want a hit. It's going to be your <u>call</u>.
Your top choices land in the shopping <u>mall</u>.

Prop Master

Creatures that scare you. Dolls that <u>talk</u>.
Monsters that grab you. Creeps that <u>stalk</u>.

They're all in the movies. And you can <u>assume</u> that the man on this page made every costume.

He's a Master of Horror. So you'd better <u>beware</u>.
He'd like nothing more than to give you a <u>scare</u>.

So go to the movies. Bring a brave <u>attitude</u>.
Remember nothing is real.
It's just the work of this <u>dude</u>!

Circus Performers

They walk on ropes. They get shot in the <u>air</u>.
They serve as targets. And you know what they <u>share</u>?

They're brave and they're fearless. No room for <u>gloom</u>.
They get to their job with a zip, <u>zoom</u>, and <u>boom</u>.

Go to the circus. So you can <u>compare</u>
which of these jobs is really a <u>scare</u>.

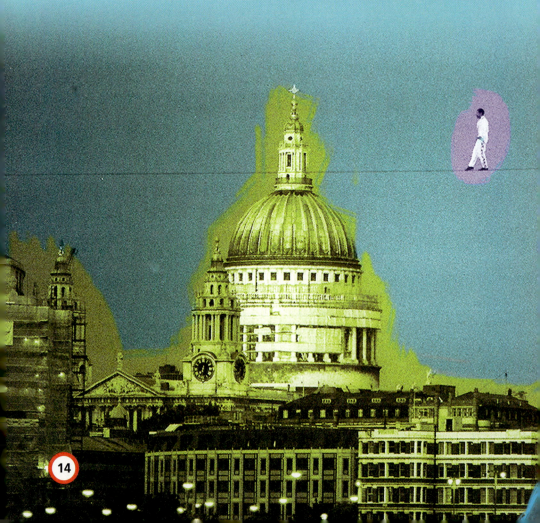

You Call That a Job?

You've read my whole book.
I <u>offer</u> much <u>gratitude</u>.

Your work is not finished.
I don't mean to be <u>rude</u>.

Which of these jobs would you like to do?
Which of these jobs are clearly not you?

Look at the list. It's time to <u>compare</u>.
You call that a job . . .

. . . or a job nightmare!

- Statue Cleaner
- Deodorant Tester
- Video Crew
- Shopping Cart Collector
- Shark Expert
- Snake Handler
- French Fry Tester
- Prop Master
- Ostrich Farmer
- Video Game Tester
- Circus Performers

Special thanks to Los Angeles teacher—and surfer—Bryan Thornton for his help with this book.